```
    P
    372.5   Forte, Imogene
            From A to Z with
            me.
```

DATE DUE			
FEB 21 '89			
MAY 22 '90			
OCT 1992			

FROM·A·TO·Z WITH ME

A SELF-CONCEPT ACTIVITY BOOK FOR YOUNG CHILDREN

*This book was
conceived and written by Imogene Forte,
taken from, added to and "fixed up" by Elaine Raphael,
designed and illustrated by Mary Hamilton.
And so,
we dedicate it
each to the other
and
to Luke.*

ISBN 0-86530-027-5

Copyright © 1981 by Incentive Publications, Inc., Nashville, Tennessee.

All rights reserved except as here noted.

All pupil activity pages are designed to be used by individual pupils. Permission is hereby granted to the purchaser of one copy of FROM A TO Z WITH ME to reproduce copies of these pages in sufficient quantity to meet the needs of the students in one classroom.

TABLE OF CONTENTS

A is for Almost, All and About 8
B is for Beagles, Bagels and Bandages 10
C is for Calendars, Clowns and Clocks 12
D is for Daffodils, Dragons and Dreams 14
E is for Ears, Eyes and the Earth 16
F is for Faces, Faults and Families 18
G is for Grand, Glorious and Grownups 20
H is for Hamburgers, Habits and Hats 22
I is for Ink, Ivy and Ice Cream 24
J is for Jungle, Jump and Just Me 26
K is for Kittens, Kisses and Kitchens 28
L is for Loving, Laughing and Listening 30
M is for Magic, Mystery and Make-Believe 32
N is for Neighbors, Numbers and Names 34
O is for Octopus, Oysters and Opinion 36
P is for People, Places and Privacy 38
Q is for Quilt, Quiet and Question 40
R is for Roses, Rainbows and Reading 42
S is for Sandwiches, Sunshine and Seasons 44
T is for Tiger, Trust and Television 46
U is for Unicycle, Umbrella and Unique 48
V is for Violins, Violets and Very Well 50
W is for Windmills, Weather and Windows 52
X is for "X marks the spot," Xylophone and X-Ray . 54
Y is for You, Yak and Yawn 56
Z is for Zebra, Zipper and Zachariah 58
A-B-Secrets 60
My Own Picture Dictionary 61

FROM A TO Z WITH ME

A Self-Awareness Activity Book for Young Children

FROM A TO Z WITH ME is made up of reproducible pupil activity pages designed to help children become more aware of themselves, of the world around them, and of their own special places in that world. Each page has been carefully planned to provide flexibility and freedom, and to enhance the child's self-concept.

The alphabet format has been utilized because of its familiarity and appeal to children. However, FROM A TO Z WITH ME is much more than an alphabet book. Every activity stands on its own to teach one or more specific reading, writing and/or reasoning skill. Each one is intended to contribute to the development of the sound skills foundation necessary for school success. Completion of these activities will give order and meaning to isolated facts and knowledge while extending the child's social insights and understanding.

Through creative involvement with the ideas and concepts presented, the child is encouraged to focus on talents and abilities, strengths and weaknesses, personality traits and personal preferences that make him or her unique and special. When shared by children and grownups in a warm and friendly setting, the activities in FROM A TO Z WITH ME should provide a springboard for questioning, for pondering, and for dreaming — the ingredients necessary for the development of positive growth in learning.

Imogene Forte
June, 1981

This book belongs to

_____

It's about
   who I am,
   where I live,
   people I know,
   what I do
     and
   how I grow.

 is for Almost, All and ABOUT...

This book is almost all about ME.
My full name is:
_____

My address is:
(Street) _____
(City) _____
(State) _____

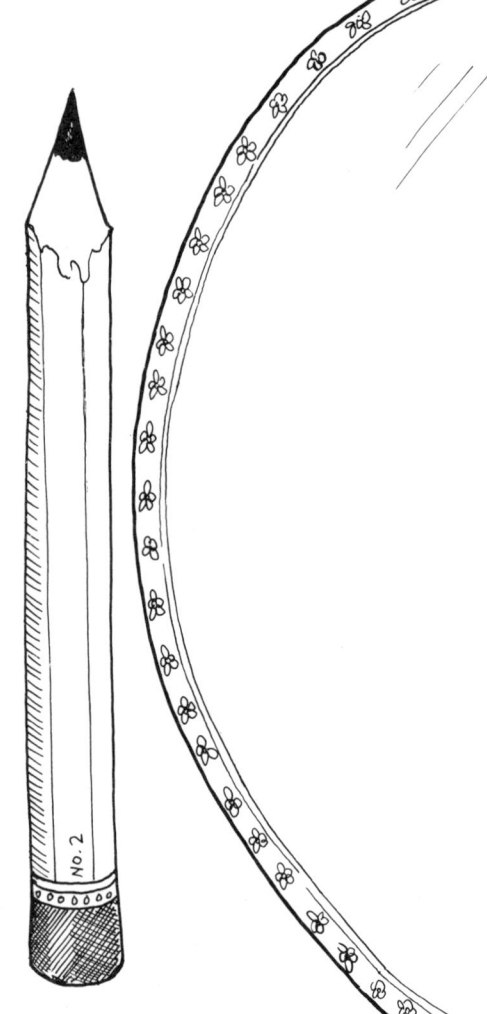

HERE I AM!

If you want to call me on the phone, use this number.

_____

This book is also about ...
    the people I know
    the home I live in
    the school I go to
    and the big, wide, wonderful
world of which I am a part.

Here they are!

B is for Beagles, Bagels and BANDAGES ...

Once in a while, I fall down and bump my head or bruise my knee.

First I cry a little.

That makes it hurt less.

Then, someone who loves me puts a bandage on the hurt place.

That makes it all better.

Here is a picture of me the last time I hurt myself.

See my bandages?

Sometimes the worst hurts you get don't even show.
Those hurts are on the inside.
You get them when someone is mean to you or hurts your feelings.
You can't put a real bandage on that kind of hurt.

Can you remember when you made someone hurt inside?
Show how you think that person felt.
What could you do to make that person feel better?

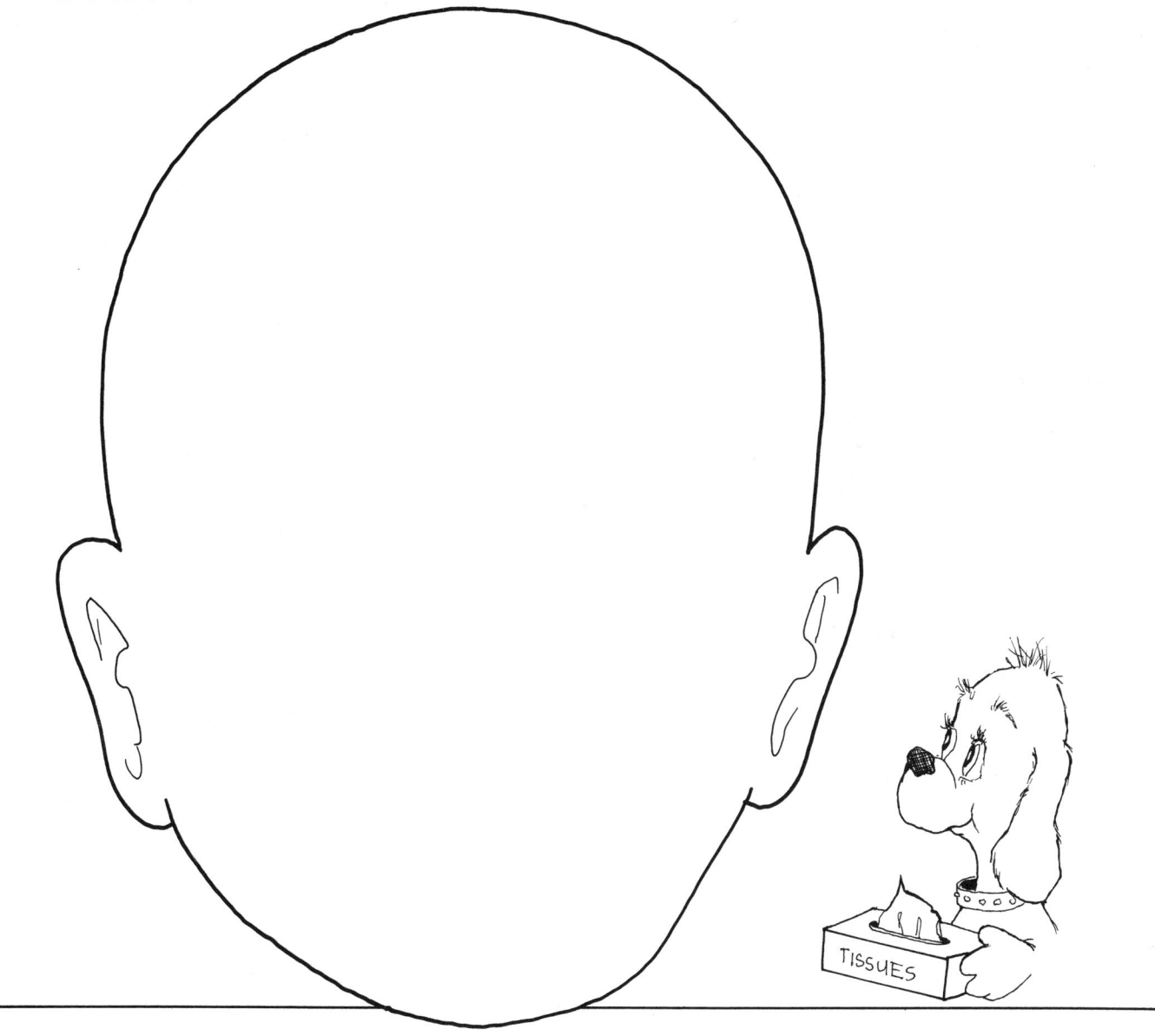

A calendar will help you find the answers to these questions.

CALENDAR

SUNDAY	MONDAY	TUESDAY	WEDNESDAY	THURSDAY	FRIDAY	SATURDAY
			1	2	3	4
5	6					

On what day of the week will your next birthday be? _____

What day of the week do you like best? _____

Why? _____

What day of the week do you like least? _____

Why? _____

How many Sundays in this month? _____

What is the most exciting day of the year for you? _____

Why? _____

D is for Daffodils, Dragons and DREAMS ...

Pretend that it's a lazy summer day. You're lying on your back looking at the clouds.

You fall asleep and dream about what you'll be when you grow up.
Show your dream.

Do you know the story of Rip Van Winkle?
He fell asleep and woke up years later to find that many changes had taken place.
Think about the changes that may take place by the time you are a grownup. Close your eyes, and daydream about this world.
Show yourself and your new world here.

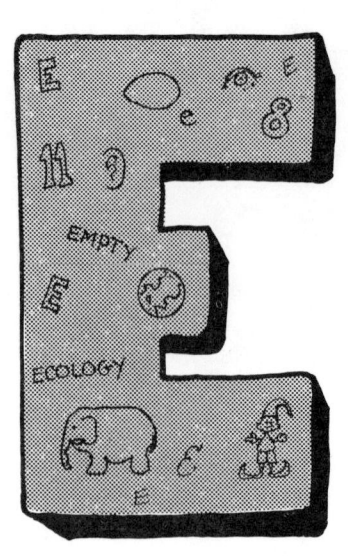 is for Ears, Eyes and the   EARTH ...

The planet Earth is your home.
It's a place where green things grow and the air is sweet.
But sometimes, litter chokes the green plants and the air smells bad because of smoke and pollution.
Show some things you can do to make your Earth a better place to live.

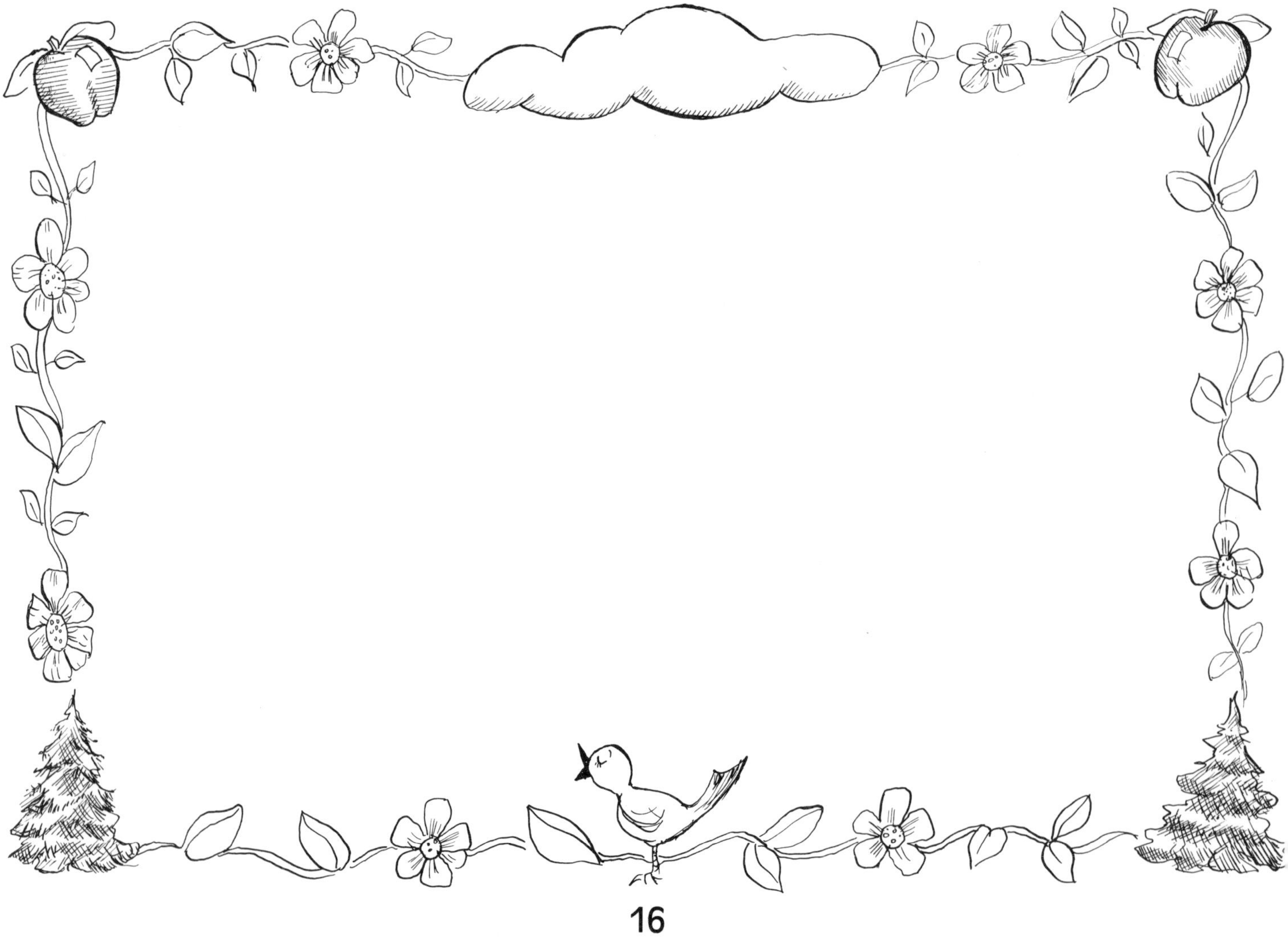

We learn about other people by using our eyes to watch them and our ears to hear what they say.

When you hear someone say nice things about you, it makes you feel good.

Do you know someone you'd like to say something especially nice to?

Who is it? _____

What would you like to say?

_____
_____
_____
_____
_____
_____
_____
_____
_____
_____
_____
_____
_____

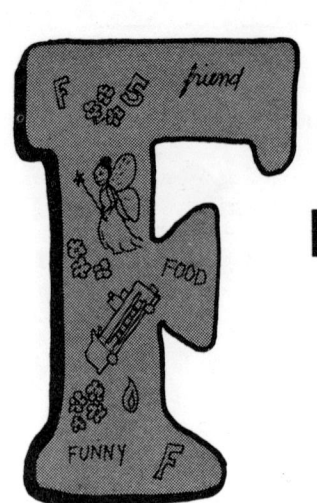 is for Faces, Faults and FAMILIES ...

Here is a picture of me with my family.

Family Portrait

Don't you think we are handsome?

There is something special about every family member.

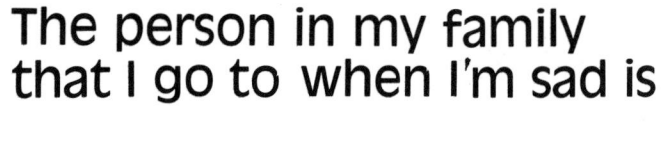

The person in my family that I go to when I'm sad is

_____

The person in my family that I like to play with is

_____

The person in my family who needs me the most is

_____

The person in my family that I'd like to take a long airplane trip with is

_____

The person in my family who makes me laugh most often is

_____

 is for Grand, Glorious and GROWNUPS ...

Sometimes it's hard
   for grownups and kids to
      understand
   each other.
Each wonders
   why the other does
      some of the things they
   do,
And each wishes
   the other
      knew.

Show something here that you do that grownups hate.

Show something here that grownups do that you hate.

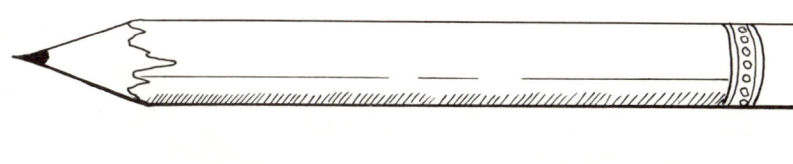

Write about or draw one thing that you aren't allowed to do now that you really look forward to doing when you are a grownup.

is for Hamburgers, Habits and HATS ...

For special days, you need special hats.

Make each hat show a special holiday.
Write the name of the holiday on the line beside each hat.

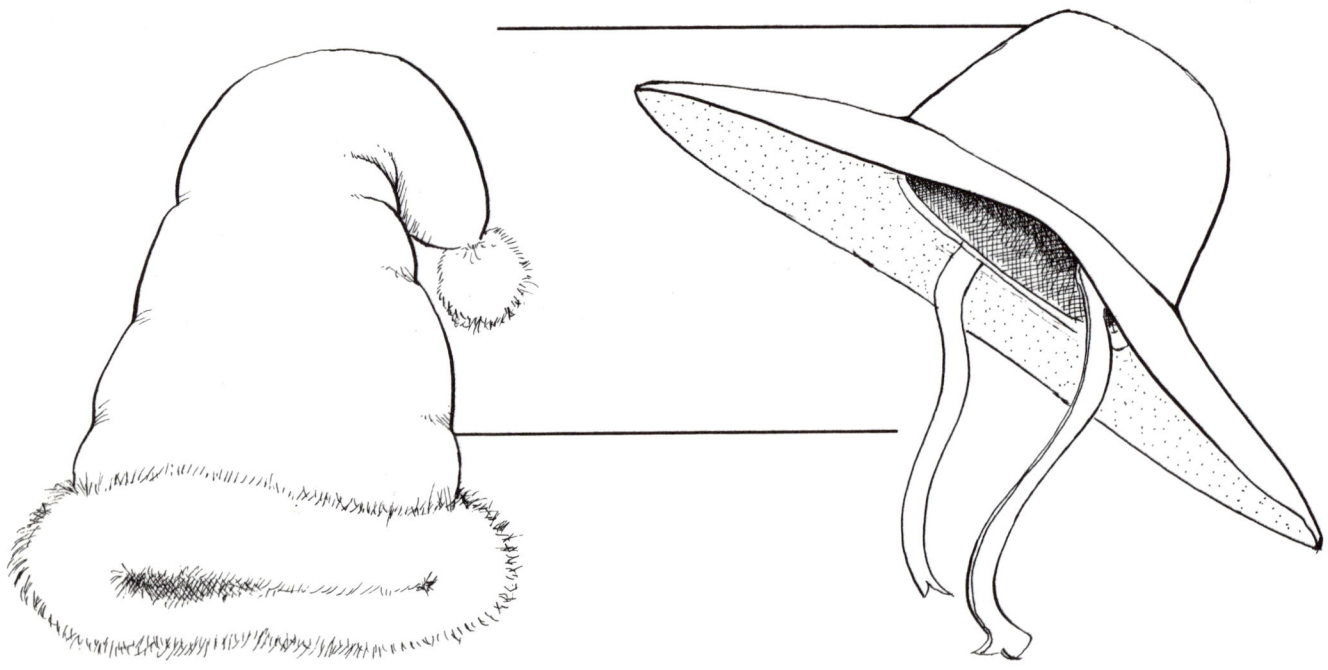

Habits are things we've done so often that we do them almost without thinking.

What's your worst habit?

Is it forgetting to turn off lights you aren't using?

Is it interrupting other people when they're talking?

Or do you always forget to put your toys away?

What good habits do you have?

Do you always remember to wash your face and brush your teeth when you should?

Are you polite and considerate of other people?

Do you keep your room neat?

Show or tell about one of your good habits here.

I is for

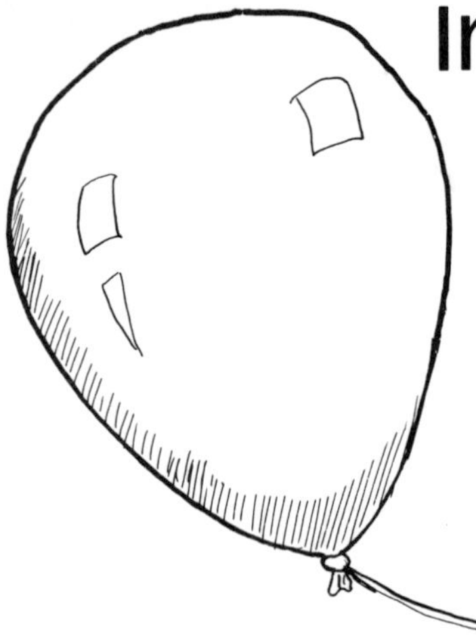

Ink,

Ivy

and

ICE CREAM ...

Plan an ice cream party for 3 people you like.

List their names.
Tell the special things that made you include them on this list.
Then, tell what flavor of ice cream you think each person would like best.

Person	Special Thing	Ice Cream Flavor
1.		
2.		
3.		

Thinking of new ways to use ordinary things helps you stretch your imagination and makes YOU "extra-ordinary."

Show 3 ways to use an ice cream cone for something other than for ice cream.

Connect the dots from 1 to 25 to frame your work.

25

J is for Jungle, Jump and JUST ME...

This story of my life
   Is short and sweet.
It's all about me
   And I think it's neat.

Just so you'll know, I'll share with you some of my favorite places.

A THINKING PLACE

A RAINY DAY PLACE

A PICNIC PLACE

A LEARNING PLACE

K is for Kittens, Kisses and KITCHENS ...

Kitchens are for kids!
What foods can you fix without any help?
On the table, show a meal that you can fix.

This kitchen is a mess!
Some of these things belong here, but others don't.
Circle the things you might use to make a meal.

Tidy up the kitchen.
Draw a line from each of the things you don't need to the basket.

 is for Loving,  Laughing and LISTENING ...

The world is full of sounds.
Some make you feel good.
Some make you feel bad.

Make a list of 3 scary sounds.
1. _____
2. _____
3. _____

Make a list of 3 comforting sounds.
1. _____
2. _____
3. _____

List 3 sad sounds.
1. _____
2. _____
3. _____

List 3 happy sounds.
1. _____
2. _____
3. _____

M is for Magic, Mystery and MAKE-BELIEVE ...

Elves and gnomes and leprechauns
Are fluttery fairy folks
Full of mystery and magic,
And make-believe and jokes.

If they gave me a magic carpet
To carry me to and fro,
This is what I'd do,
And here is where I'd go.

Remember the story of Alladin and his magic lamp? Whenever Alladin wanted something, all he had to do was rub his lamp and a genie would appear to grant his wish.

Make-believe that you own a magic lamp. Write or draw the one thing you would wish for more than anything else in the whole world.

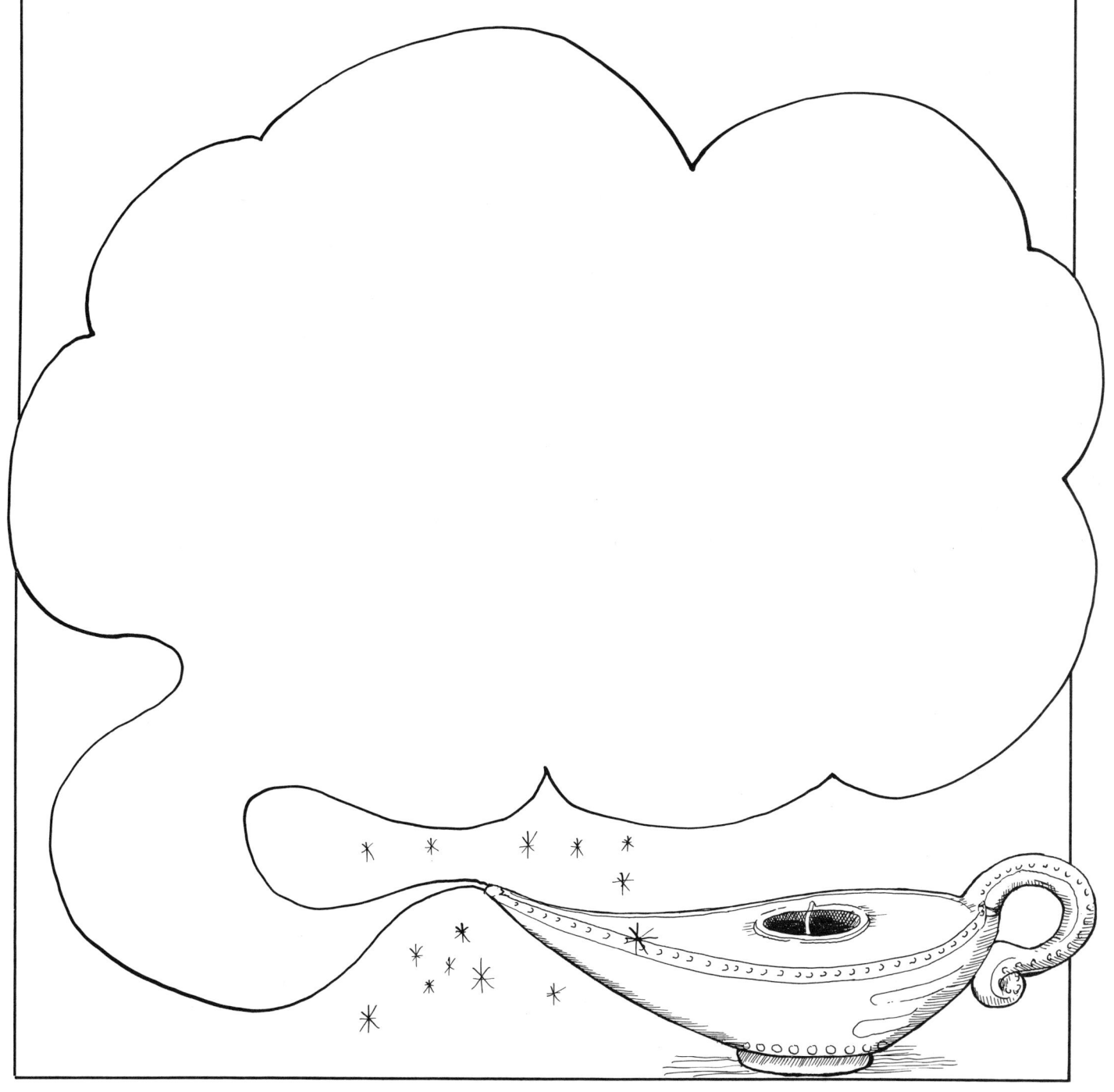

is for Neighbors, Numbers and NAMES ...

Here is my full name.

_____

I can write my name backward.

_____

I can write my name upside down.

_____

I can write my name round and round in a circle.

The important thing about my name is that it's all mine. Anytime, anywhere, any way I write my name, it belongs to me, and it tells you who I am.

Numbers tell many interesting things.

Here are some special numbers.

This number tells how many days are in a week. _____

This number tells what time school starts. _____

This number tells how many kids are in my class. _____

This number tells how much 1 + 1 is. _____

This number tells what year it is. _____

Here are all the numbers I can write.

O is for Octopus, Oysters and OPINION ...

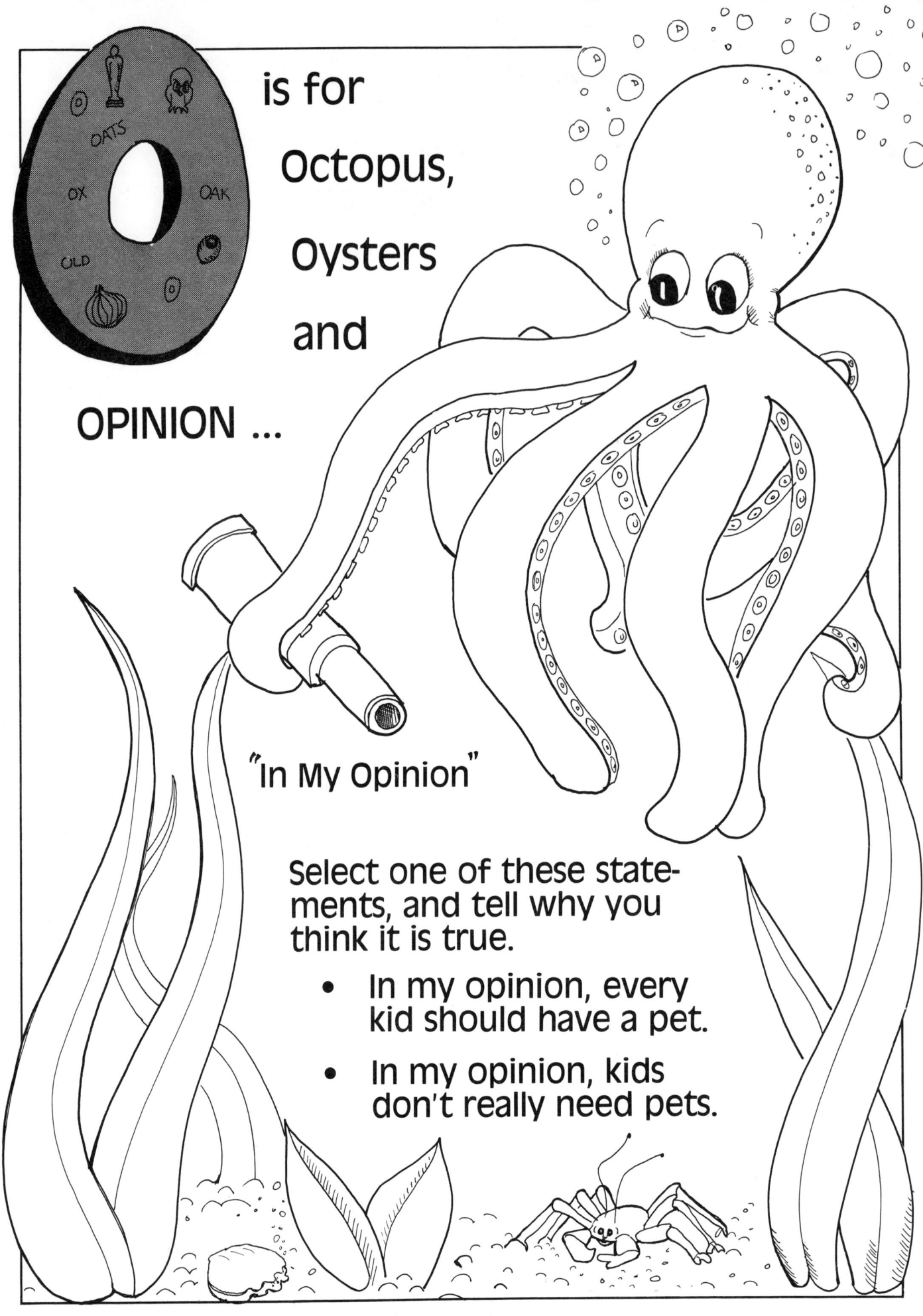

"In My Opinion"

Select one of these statements, and tell why you think it is true.

- In my opinion, every kid should have a pet.
- In my opinion, kids don't really need pets.

Ask for opinions.
Then, count the "yes" and "no" answers.
You may be surprised!

	Parent		Teacher		Friend		You	
	yes	no	yes	no	yes	no	yes	no
Kids watch too much T.V.								
Kids should watch only educational programs.								
More movies should be shown on T.V.								
Cartoon programs are time-wasters.								
People do bad things because they see them on T.V.								
Totals								

P is for People, Places and PRIVACY...

Everybody needs a little privacy sometimes.

Here are some signs you can use to let people know when you want to keep things private.

Color the signs and cut them out.

Tape them onto things as you need to.

Maybe you have a special shelf you'd like for other people to leave alone, or a special place you go when you want to be by yourself.

Every person in the world needs privacy, just as you do.

Finish these signs.

Give them to special people to show that you understand and respect their need for privacy.

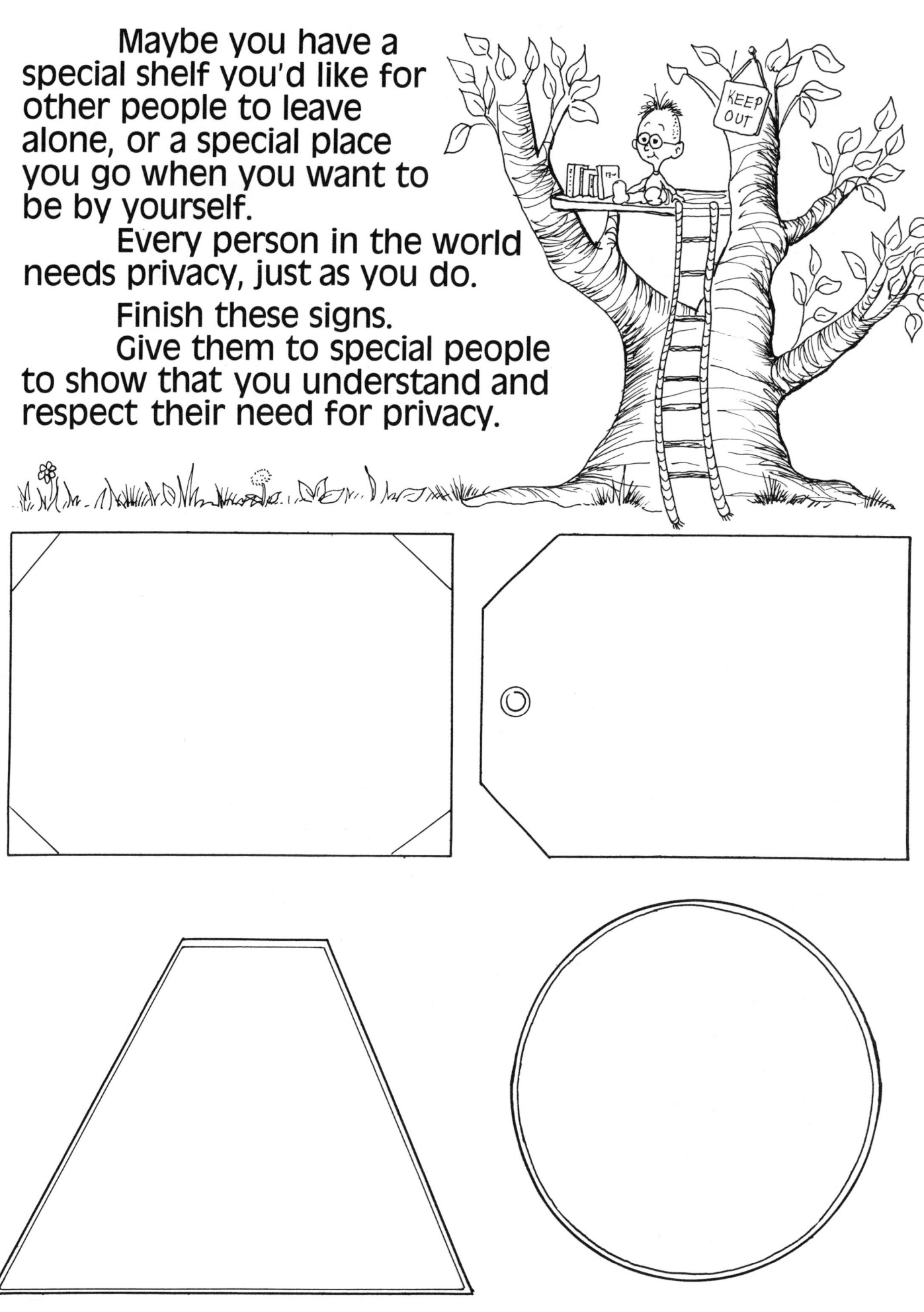

39

Q is for Quilt, Quiet and QUESTION...

Remember the story of the old man and his wife who were granted three wishes? They wasted all of them because they wished before they thought.

Sometimes people waste questions the very same way — they ask questions before they think about what they really want to know.

Write three questions that you really want answers for.

1. _____
2. _____
3. _____

Quick!
Find the answers to these "Q" questions.

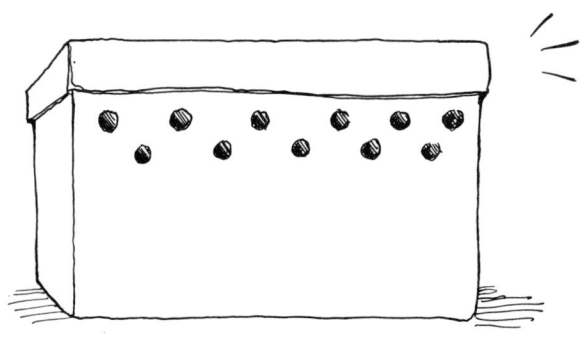

What animal says, "Quack?"
_____

How many people are in a quartet?
_____

What is quicksand?
_____
_____
_____

What does a queen wear on her head?
_____

What would you use a quill for?
_____

R is for Roses, Rainbows and READING ...

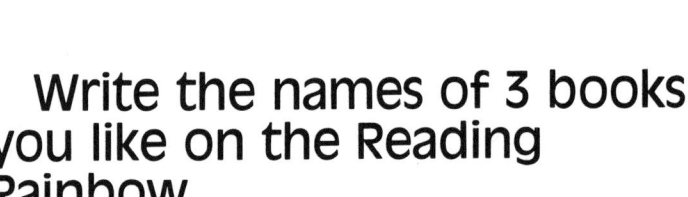

Write the names of 3 books you like on the Reading Rainbow.

Color your favorite book purple.

Color your second choice blue.

Color your third choice yellow.

Finish coloring your rainbow.

Finish these book marks.
Make one for yourself, and one for a friend.

Print your name on your book mark.
Print your friend's name on the other one.

If I had a giant sandwich,
Some cookies and milk and a game,
I'd share them all with my best friend ...
_____ is my best friend's name.

And after we'd finished eating,
And had played the game for a while,
Here are some of the other things
We'd do to make us smile!

T is for Tiger, Trust and TELEVISION ...

What do you know about your T.V. habits?
Write the names of all the television programs you watch during the next 2 days.

Think about the programs you saw and why you watched them.
What have you learned about yourself from this?

Did you ever wish that you could be one of the characters in your favorite T.V. program?

If you could be any T.V. person for just one day, who would it be?

_____

Draw a picture to show yourself doing something you'd want to do as this person.

Now, think about why you chose this person.

Write just three words to tell what you like most about this person.

_____   _____   _____

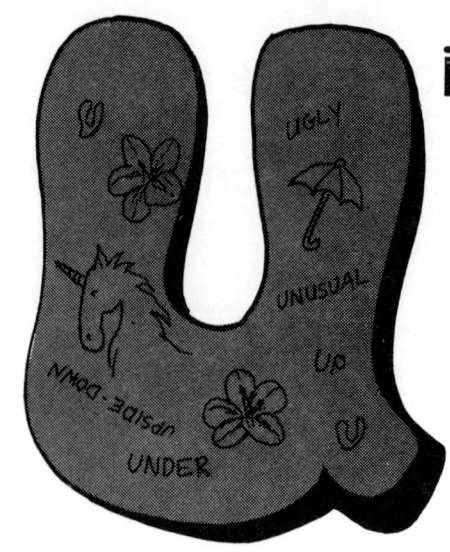 is for Unicycle,

Umbrella

and

UNIQUE ...

Unique means being the only one of a kind.

I am unique!

I'm unique because there is not one single person in the whole wide world who is exactly like me.

When I look in the mirror, I can see three things about myself that make me uniquely me.

These three things are:

1. _____

2. _____

3. _____

Of all things about me that make me unique, I'm most proud of _____

Some people like popcorn.
   Others hate peanuts.
One person I know likes
   Soup a la coconuts!

My favorite food is _____.

But I just despise _____.

Some people like baseball.
   Some people won't swim.
Some people like tennis.
   Some people hate gym.

My favorite sport is _____.

But I hate to play _____.

Some people like hot weather.
   Others like snow.
And some like rainy days
   Wherever they go.

My favorite weather is _____.

But I just hate it when it _____.

   Now that you know about some of my favorite and not-so-favorite things, you know more about why I am uniquely me.

V is for Violins, Violets and VERY WELL ...

Use your favorite crayon to check the box that shows how well you can do each of the things listed on the "Can Do" Chart.

When you have finished, ask a friend to use another crayon to do the same thing.

Then, compare the checks.

I CAN	Not Very Well	Pretty Well	Very Well
sew			
cook			
read			
write			
spell			
swim			
dance			
sing			
whistle			
draw			

What this really shows is that people are all different, and can do different things well.

Isn't that wonderful?

is for Windmills, Weather and WINDOWS ...

Every window frames a picture of the world outside.
What kind of picture does your window frame?

Pretend you are an artist. Use your crayons to show what you see.

One reason people often look out the window is to check the weather.

What kind of weather did you see outside your window today?

These sentences tell about different kinds of weather.

Read the sentences, and find the right word in the puzzle to finish each one.

Circle the words and write them in the correct blanks.

```
T H U N D E R F
F S R O M A T O
O L Z H O T W G
I E R A I N Y T
H E W I N D M E
F T R O M A T O
Z S H O W E R S
```

April ___ ___ ___ ___ ___ ___ ___ bring May flowers.

Winter storms can bring snow and ___ ___ ___ ___ ___ .

I like an ice cold drink when the weather is ___ ___ ___ .

It's hard to see through ___ ___ ___ .

In autumn, the brisk ___ ___ ___ ___ blows the dead leaves around.

I like to walk through the puddles on ___ ___ ___ ___ ___ days.

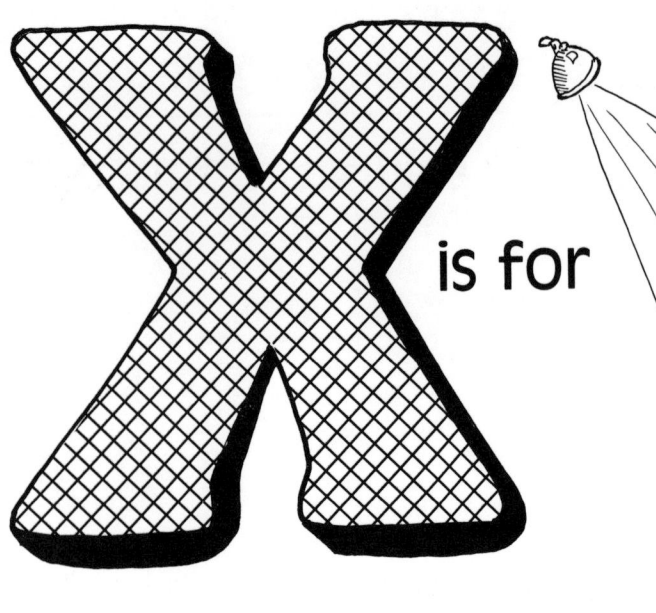 is for "X marks the spot," Xylophone and X-RAY ...

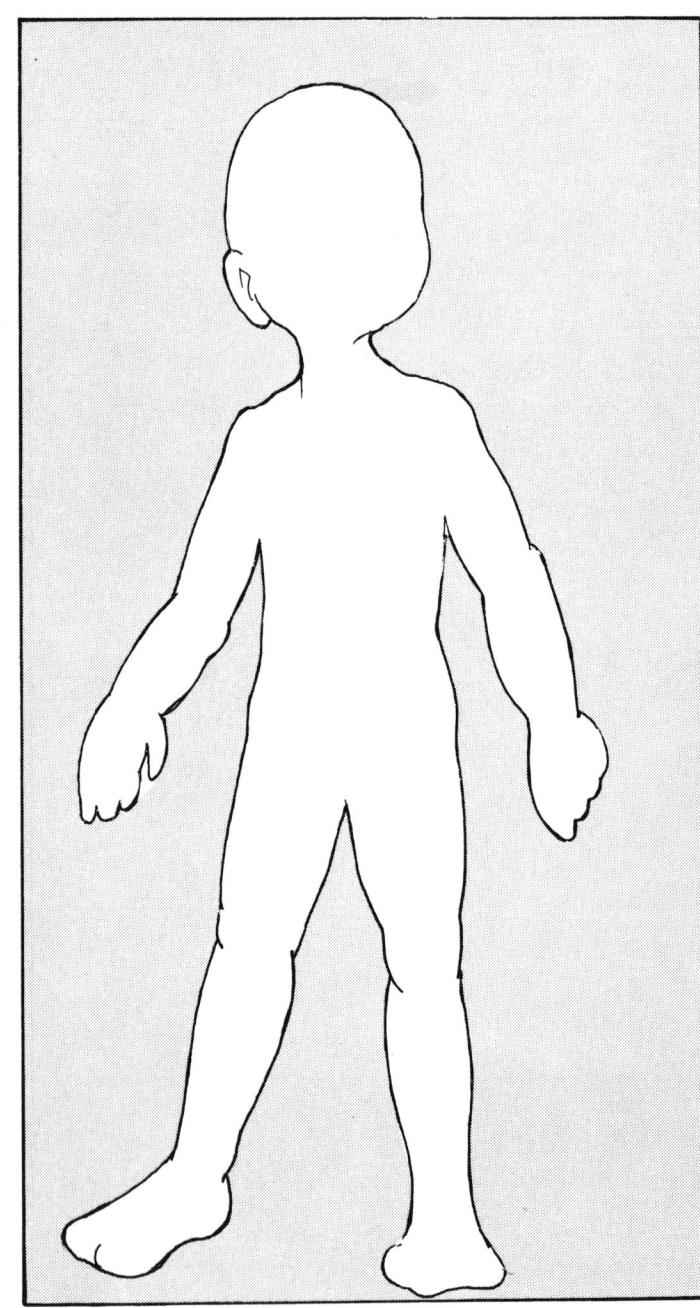

X-rays are pictures that show parts of the body which can't be seen from the outside.

Here is a list of body parts you have that you can't see.

Draw a line from each one to where you think it would show up in an X-ray.

- heart
- lungs
- kidneys
- back bone
- pelvis
- jaw bone
- shoulder bone
- intestines
- brain

Read each sentence below, and decide whether it is true or false.

Circle the letter in the correct column to find out how the doctor sees your body with an X-ray.

		True	False
1.	Your heart is in your stomach.	A	I
2.	Most people have two knees.	N	W
3.	Good eating habits build strong bodies.	S	E
4.	Your lungs are right above your feet.	G	I
5.	People normally have ten toes and ten fingers.	D	O
6.	Your jaw bone helps you walk.	F	E
7.	Your brain is where you do your thinking.	O	S
8.	Your back bone is part of your arm.	B	U
9.	Your elbow is where your arm bends.	T	C

Now, copy the circled letters here to find out how "body wise" you are.

___ ___ ___ ___ ___ ___
 1   2   3   4   5   6

___ ___ ___
 7   8   9

Y is for You, Yak, and YAWN ...

I yawn when I am bored.
I become bored when _____
_____
_____
_____
_____

But, I stop yawning and wake up when
_____
_____
_____
_____
_____

Yannie Yawn loves to stay up late at night. He often sits up after everyone else is in bed, and turns the T.V. on to watch the "Late, Late Show." But this causes a problem — he simply cannot stop yawning.

He yawns at the breakfast table. He yawns on the way to school, in the classroom and on the playground. He yawns at the circus, and even at his own birthday party.

If Yannie were my friend, I would tell him

is for Zebra, Zipper and ZACHARIAH ...

I don't know anyone named Zachariah. Do you?

Think about the names of all the people you know.

Beside each letter in the list below, write a name that begins with that letter.

A _____
B _____
C _____
D _____
E _____
F _____
G _____
H _____
I _____
J _____
K _____
L _____
M _____

N _____
O _____
P _____
Q _____
R _____
S _____
T _____
U _____
V _____
W _____
X _____
Y _____
Z _____

And while you're thinking about names, "zip off" the names of:

a person who makes you laugh
_____

a person you'd like to eat lunch with
_____

a fine teacher
_____

a person who cooks food you like
_____

a good neighbor
_____

your doctor
_____

your best friend
_____

A-B-SECRETS

> As you went from A to Z,
> How many secrets did you see?
> If you missed these, start with A
> To find what else the letters say.

Ant, apron, apple and add ...
Broom, bone, ball and boat ...
Cat, car, cup and crisp ...
Duck, dizzy, desk and dog ...
Elephant, elf, earth and eye ...
Fairy, food, flower and friend ...
Girl, grapes, goose and grumpy ...
Hint, holly, hand and hot ...
Inch, Indian, igloo and if ...
Just J!
Kettle, kerchief, know and knife ...
Lips, lock, log and like ...
Mustard, mouse, money and more ...
Nut, nose, nickel and nap ...
Oscar, onion, olive and oak ...
Pine, pail, pan and please ...
Quiet, quiet Q.
Rake, rabbit, rash and rope ...
Silly, sock, sandwich and shark ...
Thimble, thumb, top and toy ...
Unicorn, under, umbrella and up ...
Vampire, vegetable, vision and veil ...
Walnut, wagon, welcome and witch ...
X-tra X's!
Yo-yo, yummy, yellow and you ...
Zinnia, Zelda, zowie and zoom!

MY OWN PICTURE DICTIONARY

Every day, the things I see
Become a brand-new part of me.
And so, I'd like to draw right here
Pictures of things that I hold dear,

Things I love and things I do,
Things I want to share with you.
So take a moment, if you please,
And look at my own ABC's.

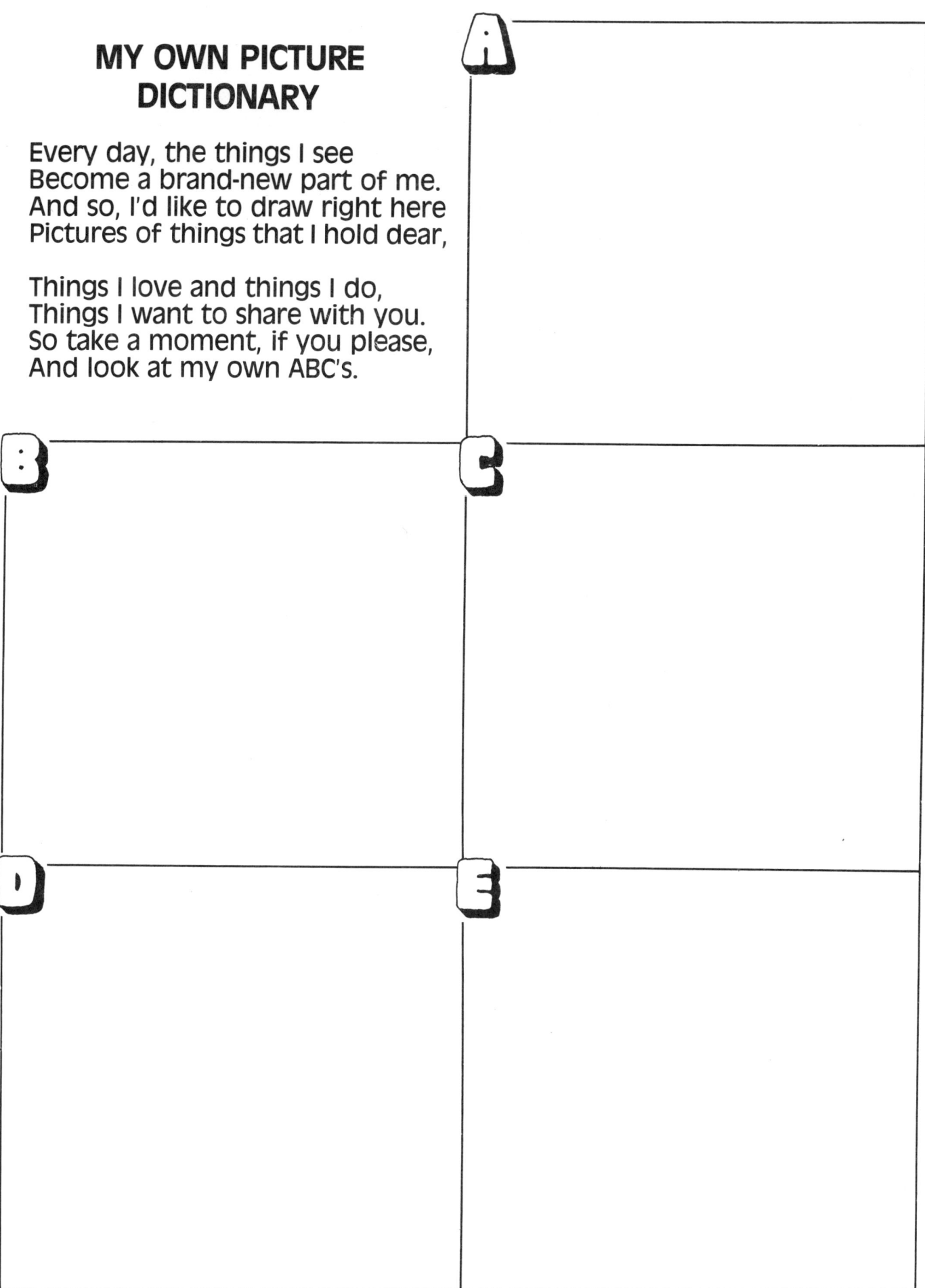

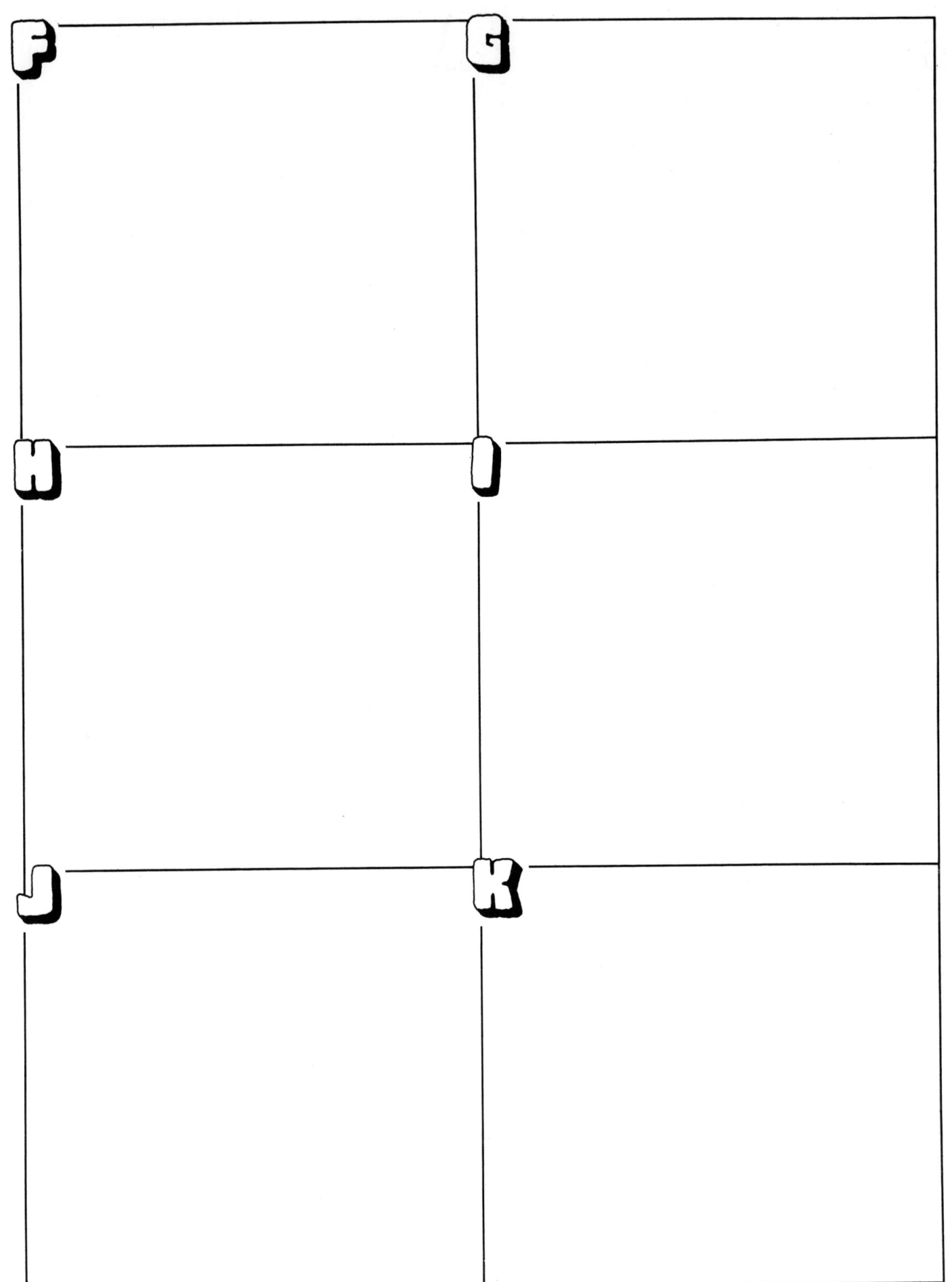